GLENN RAWSON STORIES

TELL ME THE STORIES OF

Christmas

GlennRawsonStories.com

Cover artwork *Adoration of the Shepherds* by Gerrit van Honthorst

ISBN 978-163649489-0

Printed in the United States of America

10 9 8 7 6 5 4 3 2

Table Of Contents

Prologue

My Dear Friends,

Often, when we think of the Christmas story, we turn to Luke 2 or Matthew 1, and it is right that we do. Those are powerful, eye-witness accounts of the Savior's birth. However, Christ is the Savior of all men, of all ages, from Father Adam to the final winding up scene. There is only one Savior and one name that brings salvation. It follows then that prophets and apostles, past and present, have looked to Him and wrote of Him. In so doing, they often spoke of that first Christmas, sharing insights and prophecies beyond that of Luke or Matthew.

For the most part, this book is the telling of the Christmas story throughout the whole of the scriptures. There are other stories added in, but this book is a testimony and witness of the divinity of the Lord Jesus Christ from across the ages. Feel free to use them as needed and share them with whomever you wish.

I hope I see you again somewhere in the world.

Blessings to you,

Glenn Rawson

CHAPTER ONE

The Christmas Story

"And it came to pass in those days, that there went out a decree from Caesar Augustus, that all the world should be taxed. And this taxing was first made when Cyrenius was governor of Syria. And all went to be taxed, every one into his own city. And Joseph also went up from Galilee, out of the city of Nazareth into Judaea, unto the city of David, which is called Bethlehem; (because he was of the house and lineage of David:) To be taxed with Mary, his espoused wife, being great with child" (Luke 2:1-5).

"And so it was, that, while they were there, the days were accomplished that she should be delivered. And she brought forth her firstborn son, and wrapped him in swaddling clothes, and laid him in a manger; because there was no room for them in the inn" (Luke 2:6-7).

"And there were in the same country shepherds abiding in the field, keeping watch over their flock by night. And, lo, the angel of the Lord came upon them, and the glory of the Lord shone round about them: and they were sore afraid. And the angel said unto them,

Fear not: for, behold, I bring you good tidings of great joy, which shall be to all people. For unto you is born this day in the city of David a Saviour, which is Christ the Lord. And this shall be a sign unto you; Ye shall find the babe wrapped in swaddling clothes, lying in a manger. And suddenly there was with the angel a multitude of the heavenly host praising God, and saying, Glory to God in the highest, and on earth peace, good will toward men" (Luke 2:8-14).

"And it came to pass, as the angels were gone away from them into heaven, the shepherds said one to another, Let us now go even unto Bethlehem, and see this thing which is come to pass, which the Lord hath made known unto us. And they came with haste, and found Mary, and Joseph, and the babe lying in a manger. And when they had seen it, they made known abroad the saying, which was told them concerning this child" (Luke 2:15-17).

I want you to know, this story is true.

Merry Christmas to you.

From Luke 2

CHAPTER TWO

Ahaz's Sign

The story of Christmas began long before those events in Bethlehem. Holy men and women of God looked forward to the birth of the Lord Jesus Christ virtually from the dawn of creation. This is that story.

More than 700 years before the birth of the Savior, the people of Jerusalem were frightened. Their peace was threatened by a ruthless power from the north, called Assyria, who was taking over country after country. Judah's neighbors, Ephraim and Syria, were hastily forming political alliances to guard against the threat.

Judah's king, Ahaz, refused to join the alliance, choosing instead to bargain with Assyria directly for his nation's safety. The Kings of Ephraim and Syria were angered that Ahaz and Judah would not join them and promised to invade and remove Ahaz as King. Isaiah the prophet came to Ahaz and told him not to fear the two allied kings. Don't listen to them, be at peace, and trust the Lord. But the imminent political threat was too much for the wicked Ahaz. In his heart, he would not believe it. How could he? Their doom seemed sure in spite of

Isaiah's promises. Knowing that Isaiah said, "Ask thee a sign of the Lord thy God; ask it either in the depth, or in the height above" (Isaiah 7:11). To seek signs of ourselves is evil, but when the Lord commands us to ask for one, it is evil not to. Moreover, to be told that his sign can come from the depths of hell or the heights of heaven, whatever he wants, must mean that God is very determined that this doubting man believes His promises.

Stubbornly, Ahaz refused to ask. Isaiah was disgusted with him and all his nation and said the Lord would give him a sign anyway. "Behold," He said, addressing himself now to all the nation, "a virgin shall conceive, and bear a son, and shall call His name Immanuel" (Isaiah 7:14). Immanuel means God with us. How could a virgin bear a son?

That's impossible. Yet, God did the impossible on that first Christmas when Jesus was born. But, Ahaz would not live to see the sign fulfilled.

Christ would not be born for another seven hundred years. So, why was it given? This was not just a sign to Ahaz, but to all the children of God that doubt Him and His promises. Every Christmas is a reminder that God did once and can do again the impossible.

Any of you listening to me that are troubled for any reason and seek peace, need only look at the miracle of Christmas to awaken your latent faith.

This is, ironically, the season of the coldest weather and yet for a time, the warmest hearts. When Christmas comes "God is with us" again, in our hearts, our homes, and even our music. One need only look at how our world changes this time of year to know that Christ is still in Christmas.

4

Indeed, Christmas is an everlasting sign to a doubting world that God is still with us, that He loves us, and that He can still do the impossible, this time for you and me.

CHAPTER THREE

Benjamin and the Angel

We know that an angel came to shepherds at Bethlehem with glad tidings of great joy, but did you know that another angel came with those same tidings many, many years before?

124 BC, the land of Zarahemla—King Benjamin was awakened from his sleep by an angel. He awoke and the angel was standing before him. "Awake," he said, "and hear the words which I shall tell thee; for behold, I am come to declare unto you the glad tidings of great joy" (Mosiah 3:3).

"The time cometh," the angel continued, "and is not far distant, that with power, the Lord Omnipotent who reigneth, who was, and is from all eternity to all eternity, shall come down from heaven among the children of men, and shall dwell in a tabernacle of clay, and shall go forth amongst men, working mighty miracles, such as healing the sick, raising the dead, causing the lame to walk, the blind to receive their sight, and the deaf to hear, and curing all manner of diseases.

And he shall cast out devils...and lo, he shall suffer temptations, and pain of body, hunger, thirst, and fatigue, even more than man can suffer, except it be unto death; for behold, blood cometh from every pore, so great shall be his anguish for the wickedness and the abominations of his people. And he shall be called Jesus Christ, the Son of God, the Father of heaven and earth, the Creator of all things from the beginning; and his mother shall be called Mary.

And lo, he cometh unto his own, that salvation might come unto the children of men even through faith on his name; and even after all this, they shall consider him a man, and say that he hath a devil, and shall scourge him, and shall crucify him. And he shall rise the third day from the dead; and behold, he standeth to judge the world; and behold all these things are done that a righteous judgment might come upon the children of men" (Mosiah 3:5-10).

Benjamin immediately gathered his people to the Temple, and notwithstanding his age, climbed a high tower and shared the angel's message. When Benjamin finished, he looked down across his people. They had fallen to the earth. The fear of the Lord had come upon them and they saw themselves in need of a Savior. "They all cried aloud with one voice, saying: O have mercy and apply the atoning blood of Christ... And it came to pass that after they had spoken these words the Spirit of the Lord came upon them and they were filled with joy" (Mosiah 4:1-3).

And thus is the story of Christ and Christmas. Whether before his birth or after, that story kindles faith and brings joy. Christ is joy, and above all things, is that not the reason we live?

CHAPTER FOUR

Nephi and the Tree of Life

This year as you decorate your Christmas tree, I have a story I'd like you to think about. Within the Holy Bible, there lies a great mystery. Our first parents, Adam and Eve, partook of the forbidden fruit and thereby became mortal. You remember the story. The opportunity for man to be and become began then.

However, here's the mystery: There were two trees in the Garden of Eden – The Tree of Knowledge of Good and Evil and The Tree of Life.

After partaking of the forbidden fruit, Adam and Eve were cast out of the garden, and were not allowed to return and partake of The Tree of Life. And from there, it seems as though the entire Bible is a saga of man's continued fall from that mysterious tree. What was that tree, and how do we get back to it? Well, there's the story.

Thirty-four centuries later, another great prophet saw that same Tree of Life in a vision. He described it as beautiful, white, and precious above every other tree. And of course, he wanted to know what the tree meant.

In response to his question, he was shown in vision the most beautiful woman he had ever seen. It was Mary, the mother of Jesus, who would not be born for some 600 years. The next thing he saw was Mary caught away in the Spirit of the Lord, and when he next saw her, she was bearing the Christ child in her arms.

After witnessing the scenes of Christmas, the prophet was then asked if he understood now the meaning of The Tree of Life.

"…Yea," he said in answer. "it is the love of God, which sheddeth itself abroad in the hearts of the children of men…" (1 Nephi 11:22).

You see? The Tree of Life was a representation of God's love, and Christ's birth was the gift given to us of that love. Thus, Christmas is all about man's return to The Tree of Love. Christ came to lead us back to the love of God. There is nothing in this world that is more powerful, more pure, more precious, and more desirable to any of us than to partake of the love of almighty God through Jesus Christ. That love is so powerful, it is life itself. To have that love, to feel that love is to live, and to live without that love is only to exist.

Now, do you understand? Christmas has always been, and still is, all about love – God for His Son, the Son for us, and us for each other. This year, this Christmas, I hope that the gift of charity, that perfect, pure, and unfailing love, may take root in your heart and become a Tree of

Life – that reaches toward Heaven and spreads over your family and friends.

You know, now that I think about it, somehow it seems fitting that the symbol at the center of our Christmas is an evergreen tree.

Merry Christmas, and much love.

CHAPTER FIVE

Why the Angels Sang

On the night Jesus was born, the Angel of the Lord announced His coming and told the shepherds how to find him. "And suddenly there was with the angel a multitude of the heavenly host praising God and saying, Glory to God in the highest and on earth peace, good will toward men" (Luke 2:13-14).

I can just imagine on that holy night an innumerable chorus of angels, standing by, so filled with joy and anticipation that they burst forth in songs of praise and adoration. Heaven sang while earth slept. Clearly, they understood something we did not. The angels not only knew what Jesus would be, but what he had been.

Jesus, or Jehovah, as he was known before he was born, was in the beginning with the Father. He was the firstborn of all our Father's children and was his beloved and chosen from the beginning.

So faithful and valiant was He that even before He was born, He was like unto God. He was so much like the Father that he was called the Father.

Not just this world, but worlds without number Jesus created. He was God, the Lord omnipotent, creator of heaven and earth, and all things that in them are; the God of the Old Testament.

It was He, under the direction of the Father, who guided Enoch to build Zion. It was He who gave the law to Moses. It was He who taught the Gospel of God to the prophets from Adam to John. He was the Messenger of the Covenant, the Prince of Peace, the King of Glory, the great I AM, enthroned in power, might, majesty, and dominion. He was greater than us all, even before he was born.

From the beginning, he was that spiritual rock that led the children of God to salvation, and yet, He was as meek and lowly as a lamb. Indeed, from the beginning, Jesus prepared himself to die the sacrificial lamb that we might live. And all men from Adam to Christ exercised faith and received the benefits of an atonement that would happen, just as we exercise faith in the very one that did. And who can say why, but after creating worlds without number, Jehovah would come to this world to work out the infinite and eternal atonement.

The God of Heaven was coming here to take a mortal body. The God of glory stripped himself and came to earth as a tiny babe to work out his salvation and ours.

The Savior and Redeemer of worlds without number was born that night in Bethlehem. The heavens understood who he was and what he was and what he would do, and they could not be restrained from singing.

The more we know Him, the more we too feel constrained to sing in praise.

CHAPTER SIX

Mary, the Mother of Jesus

Mary was of the royal house of God. She was a princess by birth. She was a woman of prophecy. Her identity, mission, and name were known hundreds of years before she was born. She was more beautiful and fair than any woman of her day. She was of sufficient spiritual capacity to be transfigured and stand in the presence of God and angels.

She was favored above all women, of all time. It was she who was selected above the billions to be the mother of God's only Begotten Son. Of sufficient stature was she that when Gabriel came to her he did obeisance to her and Mary wondered why an angel would salute her so.

She was chosen to be the mother of the greatest man who would ever live. He was born to be the greatest King in this world's history and she was chosen to help Him. She was chosen to have a relationship with the God of Heaven, different from any other. When she said, "Be it unto me according to thy word" (Luke 1:38), Mary accepted a responsibility and burden the like of which no woman has ever known.

15

What a trial it must have been for this chaste and modest young woman to have anyone think of her as an adulteress. In an ecstasy of spirit with Elizabeth, Mary praised the Lord with a profundity and power that has few equals in scripture.

Meekly, Mary bore the difficult journey to Bethlehem when her time was full. There is no scriptural record that this remarkable woman ever weakened or complained of all that she was called to bear. Some mothers tend to overprotect, but not Mary. She understood from the beginning that this child was for the world. When the shepherds came in from the field, she let them see Him.

From the beginning and throughout her life, she sacrificed her name, reputation, will, wants, and personal comfort for her son. It is a law of God that commensurate with great blessings are great trials. I believe Mary was tried in mortality as no other woman has ever been. In the temple, Simeon promised her that her Son would be the subject of persecution and would one day meet the point of a sword; yet there is no evidence that she shrank back from the challenge of standing by Him throughout His life. She was true to Him until death.

After all that Mary had witnessed of the miraculous, it speaks to her spiritual maturity that she kept sacred secrets, and could thus be trusted by God. Mary was obedient; a woman of the law. Though her Son would fulfill the Law of Moses, yet she still complied with it. Though Mary had been the woman on whom God had bestowed such infinite favor, yet she was faithful and obedient to the leadership of her beloved husband Joseph. She followed him in flight into Egypt and eventually to Nazareth where they settled.

In the spirit of worship, she came up to Jerusalem every year for the feast of the Passover. On one of these trips, she and Joseph lost Jesus for several days. Can you imagine how it must have anguished her when they couldn't find Him? "Oh my, we lost the Son of God."

Mary bore at least six more children. At the marriage in Cana, Mary presided over the festivities and when they ran out of wine she demonstrated an implicit faith in her perfect Son. It is worthy of note the tenderness and loving relationship between Mary and her Son. Contrary to what appears in some scriptural texts, He was never unkind, dismissive, or disrespectful of her. She was of queenly nobility to Him. In terrible pain, she was at His bleeding feet when He hung on the cross, and resigned herself into the care of John the Beloved at her Son's request.

But, where was Joseph? Could it be that with all that she has borne, now too, she is a widow? We know very little that we can trust of her last years, but we know enough of the first 50 years of her life to declare with certainty that the trust placed in her by a loving Heavenly Father was deserved. Mary was called and foreordained from before the world's creation. Of all our Father's daughters, she stands supreme as the most faithful and powerful of them all. Someday we will more fully know how noble and great she really was. She was and is a holy woman of God!

CHAPTER SEVEN

The Christmas Wreath

The other day something occurred to me that entirely changed my perspective on Christmas. It started with something a young friend of mine said.

He said, "Christmas should mean everything the Savior means."

Now that's a simple statement, but it has a profound meaning.

And then it occurred to me that if prayer is the hour of the day each day when we remember the Savior, and our church meetings are the hours of our weekly remembrance, well, then Christmas is the season of our yearly remembrance. Christmas is like a sacramental season in which we remember the Savior, and His love and sacrifice. So in that spirit, may I share this story?

As a young man, Jeff came from a childhood of affluence. For him, Christmas meant thousands of dollars worth of presents under the tree for the family. He loved to see

Christmases like the ones that he remembered where each child had fifteen presents under the tree.

Then, his life was turned upside down! When he was twelve, his parents divorced, and during that time, life became a struggle for survival. After three years, his mother remarried a man whose wealth was great, but not in money, faith, and love. Added to Jeff and his four siblings were eight of Jack's children. Mom's budget for their first Christmas was $130.00 – $10.00 for each of thirteen children.

Well, that was an adjustment. Jeff was angry. $10 worth of gifts? Ha, this was not a real Christmas!

And then, something happened again. On Christmas Eve, all the family loaded up in an old used bus to go caroling. One of their stops that night was a place called Paradise Ranch. As Jeff and his family were a model of having not, the Raymonds were a model of having – a private golf course, three private lakes with private fishing, and boating. They had much. It was indeed a paradise!

Well, Jeff and his family's joyous caroling interrupted the Raymond's Christmas party. And so, the Raymond's and their guests came outside on the deck and listened to the family's caroling. But you know, no one can listen very long to a Christmas carol without joining in. Soon they were all singing. And then it wasn't long before something as holy as Christmas itself descended upon that little gathering. Mrs. Raymond began to cry, and soon each of them was in tears.

As Jeff and his family began to sing "Silent Night, Holy Night," Mrs. Raymond reached up and took down a very expensive wreath, and she hung it around Jeff's neck.

A change came over that young man at that point that has lasted from that day to this. Christmas was no longer the price of the gifts. It was the spirit of love and giving. There was a dawn of redeeming grace within him.

Now, today, many years later, and with travels all over the world, Jeff and his family still have and still cherish that wreath. It has become a symbol of the love, and the sacrifice, and the sharing that is Christmas.

May it be so with you, and Merry Christmas to you.

Adapted from an experience by Jeffery Clark Bettinger

CHAPTER EIGHT

The Annunciation to Mary

Knowing that we mortals tend to resist change, our Father in Heaven wisely prepares us before critical decisions are to be made by schooling our feelings and informing our agency. In that light, consider what happened to Mary, the Mother of Jesus.

"And in the sixth month the angel Gabriel was sent from God unto a city of Galilee named Nazareth" (Luke 1:26). Gabriel is Noah of the flood. He is one of heaven's presiding officers and the herald angel of great announcements.

He was sent "to a virgin espoused to a man whose name was Joseph of the House of David, and the virgin's name was Mary" (Luke 1:27). By merciful providence, Mary was not to be alone to bear God's Son. Joseph, of kingly descent, was Mary's chosen companion and protector.

The angel "came in unto her, and said, Hail, thou that art highly favored. The Lord is with thee, blessed art thou among women" (Luke 1:28). Mary stands preeminent—chosen and blessed because of her faith. Rightly, her name means "exalted." And to our Father in Heaven, she is precious.

"And when she saw him, she was troubled at his saying and cast in her mind what manner of salutation this should be" (Luke 1:29). The sight of the angel frightened and confused her. Why was he greeting her with such reverence?

"Fear not, Mary: for thou hast found favor with God. And thou shalt conceive in thy womb and bring forth a son and shalt call his name Jesus" (Luke 1:30-31). Motherhood is the highest, holiest calling on earth, but to be the mother of Jesus the Christ, He would be as He was named--His name means Savior.

"He shall be great, and shall be called the Son of the Highest: and the Lord God shall give unto Him the throne of His Father David, and He shall reign over the house of Israel forever, and of His kingdom, there shall be no end" (Luke 1:32-33). This promise must have stayed with her for the rest of her life. No matter the mortal realities, her Son was a Prince—the Prince of Peace, worlds without end. No son ever brought more honor and glory to his mother than did Jesus.

But to have a son and be not married—"How shall this be," Mary said, "seeing I know not a man" (Luke 1:34). Mary did not as yet comprehend who and what her Son was to be.

"The Holy Ghost shall come upon thee," Gabriel taught, "and the power of the Highest shall overshadow thee, therefore also that Holy Thing that shall be born of thee shall be called the Son of God" (Luke 1:35). This Son was to be like no other before or after—He was the only son God ever sired into mortality—the Only Begotten in the Flesh. The Son of God Himself was coming to earth and she was to prepare His physical tabernacle and be His Mother.

And then as if to further confirm her overwhelmed faith— "And thy cousin Elizabeth, she hath also conceived a son in her old age, and this is the sixth month with her who was called barren. For with God nothing shall be impossible" (Luke 1:36-37). When all the powers of hell would be let loose on Mary and her family, she would always remember and know—God can do the impossible. What serenity and peace this proven truth must have been to her.

The call was explained and extended, her calling and election in mortality was offered. "Now...Behold, the handmaid of the Lord," Mary said in meek submission, "Be it unto me according to thy word" (Luke 1:38). Notably, before Jesus would say, "Not my will but thine be done" (Luke 22:42), His Mother, in principle, would say it first.

Besides her Son, did any mortal ever accept so much with so few words? My soul overflows with reverence and awe for Mary—what manner of woman was she, is she? And how did Heaven consider her? I can't even find the words.

CHAPTER NINE

Alma, the Younger

What is the true meaning of Christmas? I hear a lot of people ask that. Well, I guess that depends upon what Christ means to you. I've concluded that the more we know Christ, the more we will truly understand Christmas. To me, this true story represents the heart of Christmas.

There was once a man named Alma the Younger. He was the son of a righteous father, Alma. Alma had made great sacrifices for his faith, but for some reason, the son became bitter and turned against the religion of his father.

Alma the Younger became a powerful and persuasive anti-Christ. As his father labored to build faith and spiritual strength, Alma the Younger became a spiritual murderer, traveling about the land destroying the faith and testimony of many. He was described as the vilest of sinners.

Then one day an unusual thing happened: An angel of the Lord appeared and spoke with a voice so thunderous and powerful that it shook the earth under this young man's feet, and knocked him to the ground. Alma was then commanded by the angel to stand up and told that if he did not stop his persecutions, he would be 'cast off' to hell. It was the last thing he would hear.

For three days and three nights, this young man was tortured in the most extreme manner by a bright recollection of all his sins. His pains and his guilt were of the most exquisite degree. The very thought he said of coming into the presence of God racked his soul with inexpressible horror. He wished that he could become extinct, body and soul.

From the midst of this self-inflicted damnation, Alma remembered the teachings of his father concerning Jesus and His Atonement. He cried out in the anguish of his soul, "…O Jesus, thou Son of God, have mercy on me…" (Alma 36:18).

No sooner had he thought this, than he could remember his sins no more, his pain and guilt were swept away and replaced with an exquisite and sweet joy. The intensity of his repentance caused him to experience a mighty change of heart. He was born again, and under the tutelage of a loving Savior, he became a righteous and holy man.

Alma the Younger, this vilest of sinners, became through the miracle of Christ and the Atonement, a mighty prophet. So faithful was he, that at the end of his life, Alma was taken to heaven without tasting death, and from his sons and grandsons came a line of prophets and record-keepers lasting over 400 years.

My friends, Christmas is the gift of a Savior who is mighty to save. I add my witness that He was born to die and rise again. He lives, and the greatest gift we can give any man is to lead him to a Savior who will give him all. (Based on the Life of Alma the Younger found in Mosiah 27 and Alma 36)

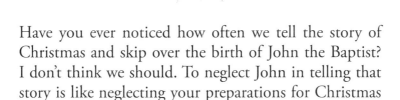

CHAPTER TEN

Bethlehem and John the Baptist

Have you ever noticed how often we tell the story of Christmas and skip over the birth of John the Baptist? I don't think we should. To neglect John in telling that story is like neglecting your preparations for Christmas until the morning of.

Before there was John the Baptist, there was John the baby.

Before Matthew, Mark, Luke, and John wrote of Jesus, John the Baptist kept a record first. As in his life, John pointed people to Jesus, so too did he in his birth.

Before Gabriel came to Mary he appeared to an old man named Zacharias in the Temple. "Fear not, Zacharias," he said, "thy prayer is heard; and thy wife Elizabeth shall bear thee a son, and thou shalt call his name John" (Luke 1:13). The angel promised that this little boy would bring much joy to many people, but not just because he was a baby, but because he would "be great in the sight of the Lord.... Many of the children of Israel shall he turn to the Lord their God"(Luke 1:15-16), Gabriel prophesied. John would go before the Savior and "...make ready a people prepared for the Lord" (Luke 1:17).

Zacharias struggled to believe what he was hearing. I don't blame him! Elizabeth was an old woman. Nonetheless, Mary's miraculous conception was not the first. Before Mary went into hiding with a child she couldn't explain, Elizabeth was there.

One day, a beautiful young woman sent by an angel came into the courtyard of Elizabeth's home and called out a greeting. In the womb, John leaped for joy, and he and his mother were filled with the Holy Ghost. It is sublime that at that moment John bore witness of the Messiah before he even had a voice. The two sons of prophecy and their sainted mothers spent the next three months together.

As John prepared the way for Jesus, so Elizabeth prepared and consoled Mary. Before the people heard the shepherd's witness of a coming Messiah, they were astonished at the new voice and testimony of Zacharias.

His prophecies resonated through the hills and hearts of the Jews, filling them with grand expectations. Then and later, all who ever knew John couldn't wait to meet Jesus.

On the night of the Savior's birth in Bethlehem, John was three months old in Hebron. Knowing what Elizabeth knew of Mary and the bond they shared, I wonder how far away she really was from her young cousin.

When Herod's soldiers came, you know they were looking for two famous babies—not one.

While the angel sent Joseph and Mary into Egypt to save Jesus, Zacharias sent John and Elizabeth into the wilderness. Joseph and Jesus escaped, but the soldiers killed Zacharias. He would not give up his son. As Jesus grew up with his Father, hewing wood, so John grew up in the wilderness eating locusts and wild honey. As Jesus waited and prepared to bring men to His Father, so John waited and prepared to bring men to Jesus.

As Luke's story of Christmas tells of a special babe whose birth pointed men to Jesus' birth—as John was born to prepare the way--may we be reminded this Christmas that we, too are born to prepare the way. The Messiah is coming—soon. God grant that we be like John, that in all that we are, all that we say, all that we do, men want to meet Him.

Joseph

You know, as a baby, the Lord Jesus was as weak and vulnerable as any other child ever born. And so in the wisdom of God, a man was chosen as a protector of the Christ-child and His mother. That man was Joseph, the carpenter. I want to talk about Joseph for a few minutes.

There's a principle that says, "Where much is given, much is required." Joseph was blessed with the love and the hand of the most beautiful maiden in all the land.

Mary was a precious and chosen young woman. Yet, he was also entrusted to protect her and shepherd the development of God's only Begotten Son. It was not a small trust.

Now, consider the following the next time you read the story about Joseph.

Obedient to the angel, Joseph married Mary and named her child Jesus. What if Joseph had been an extremist and decided to have her stoned as an adulteress? Obedient to the law, Joseph returned to Bethlehem to be taxed with

Mary, his wife, and thus he fulfilled prophecy. What if he'd refused, and the trip was never made?

Devotedly, upon arriving in Bethlehem, Joseph sought the best for Mary in the delivery of her child, going to numerous inns. But since no one would make them room, at least he found a stable– and faithfully, Joseph brought Jesus and Mary to the Temple to do for them, after the Savior's birth, according to the requirements of the law of Moses. It was there that Simeon and Anna met them and thus fulfilled God's promise to the aged Simeon. What if Joseph had never come?

And the wise men—humbly and appreciatively, Joseph accepted the gifts offered by them. What if he had been too proud to take charity – what then?

Just imagine how the course of history would have been altered if Joseph had been slow to wake up, and slow to obey when the angel came and warned him of the approach of Herod's murderous soldiers?

Joseph was submissive to God. He fled into a strange land, taking Mary and the baby, and remained there until the angel bid him return.

True to his role, through the Savior's boyhood, Joseph taught Jesus the trade of a carpenter and loved Him deeply enough to seek Him, sorrowing for many days when He disappeared in Jerusalem at the age of twelve.

Now consider this: when the Savior hung upon the cross at the end of His life, He committed the care of His beloved mother into the hands of John the Beloved, one of the apostles. So, where was Joseph? Well, we don't know for sure. Maybe it was the death of Joseph that perfected the

Savior's empathy sufficient to bring Him to tears at the death of His friend, Lazarus, or moved Him to restore the life of the daughter of Jairus and the son of the widow of Nain, and enables Him now to comfort us when we lose those that we love. He understands perfectly.

Isaiah spoke of the Savior as "… a man of sorrows, and acquainted with grief…" (Isaiah 53:3). Surely Joseph, who loved Him, could no more have escaped the pain that his son suffered than a parent who sees his child suffer now.

Joseph, the carpenter, blessed not only the lives of Jesus and Mary with his faith and devotion, but indeed all of history. Thanks be to God for the man Joseph and the gifts he gave. May we all so live and return such gifts to the Savior now.

CHAPTER TWELVE

The Birth

I want to tell a familiar story with this in mind: Christmas is all about love.

"And it came to pass in those days, that there went out a decree from Caesar Augustus, that all the world should be taxed " (Luke 2:1).

You know, as Caesar and the oppressive Roman Empire counted and taxed the goods of life from its subjects, ("And this taxing was first made when Cyrenius was governor of Syria", Luke 2:2), at the same time a true king was born, who would also number His sheep, but would free them and give them the abundance of life, not take it.

Sometimes I wonder what that's in there for. But the book of Luke was a letter written to a friend. This parenthetical comment was directed by Luke to his friend Theophilus to give him a point of time reference for the beginning of his story.

Another thought is that every year we send Christmas cards with expressions of love and faith and greeting. So, what does that make the Book of Luke then? – the world's first Christmas card?

"And all went to be taxed, every one unto his own city. And Joseph also went up from Galilee, out of the city of Nazareth, unto Judaea unto the city of David, which is called Bethlehem; (because he was of the house and lineage of David:) To be taxed with Mary his espoused wife, being great with child" (Luke 2:3-5).

No matter what the customs of the Jews, Joseph and Mary returned to Bethlehem because God wanted them to, because Jesus had to be born in Bethlehem to fulfill the words of the prophets. We can only imagine how arduous that journey must have been for Mary, who was full-term. Yet sacrifice, then and now, brings forth the blessings of Heaven.

"And so it was, that, while they were there, the days were accomplished that she should be delivered. And she brought forth her firstborn son,…" (Luke 2:6-7).

Jesus was Mary's firstborn, and the birthright son of Joseph's family. Later, Mary would have at least four more sons and at least two daughters. So I guess you could say in more ways than one, Jesus stood at the head of a large family.

"… and wrapped him in swaddling clothes,…" (Luke 2:7).

To swaddle was to wrap the newborn to provide comfort and security. Isaiah prophesied in the Old Testament that a virgin would conceive and bring forth a son. And then he said right after that, that "…Butter and honey shall he eat…" (Isaiah 7:12-15), meaning the son of the virgin. Butter and honey were staples in the diet of the poor. The meaning seems to be that Jesus would be born in poverty. Swaddling clothes were strips of cloth, or if you will, rags.

"… and laid him in a manger; because there was no room for them in the inn[s]" (Luke 2:7).

Mary's condition would have been obvious. Imagine if an expectant mother came to your door. Could you ever turn her away? Yet in the hardness of their hearts, no one would make room for her in the inns.

Descended from the royal courts on high, the Prince of Peace, the King of Heaven, was born in His own city, among His own people, in a stable.

When Jesus said, "…I came unto mine own, and mine own received me not…" (D&C 6:21), even in His birth, it was fulfilled. Bethlehem marked the beginning of the journey for the Savior, who would descend below all things that He might rise above all things.

My friends, I hope – I hope with all of my heart that the love of the Savior fills your heart this Christmas, and that love spreads to all men as you make room for Him.

Merry Christmas.

CHAPTER THIRTEEN

The Music of Christmas

On that first Christmas night, as Joseph attended and Mary gave birth, numerous concourses of angels waited in joyful anticipation of the blessed event. And as He came into the world, they broke forth in songs of pure joy and praise to God. Never before in the history of this world has the birth of any one baby meant so much to so many.

I have often wondered where in eternity I was that night. I don't know. Maybe we were all there. I can't think of any place more important we could have been.

I have a friend who shared with me a special experience and gave me permission to tell it.

She grew up in a non-religious home. As she married and started a family, it began to weigh upon her that she wanted her children to have the kind of values that came with religious training.

At first, she tried sending her children to church, but she soon recognized the futility of that. Not a member of the church, she began attending faithfully with her own children, even being asked to sing in the choir.

One evening, one of the leaders of her congregation came to her home and was visiting with her husband. After a few minutes, they called her in and told her that the visitor had something important to share with her. Soberly and carefully, he explained that as she had been singing in the choir earlier that day, the Spirit of the Lord had whispered to him that she had been part of the angelic choir that heralded the birth of the Christ child.

Now she stood dumbfounded by his words. Such a thing had never entered her mind. Could they be true? As the years have passed, she has come to accept on faith what he said. Someday she will know more surely.

Now, my friends, I don't know if we were there. But that's not the point.

Music is the language of the Gods. We have no idea of the beauty and the harmony of the music that awaits us in our Heavenly home. It is one of the highest forms of praise and a powerful means of spiritual communication – "even like unto prayer," our Heavenly Father says.

Remember – and please remember this: When this earth was created, we sang and shouted for joy. When our Savior and Redeemer was born, we sang for joy. And, my dear friends, choirs are preparing even now for the Savior's second coming.

This Christmas, join the angels and sing! Sing like you have never done so before – the joyful music of the season.

Sing the sacred music of Christmas, and it will be with you as though you had been there. The joy and peace of Christ will fill you as it filled the angels that first night. God bless you and Merry Christmas!

CHAPTER FOURTEEN

The Wise Men

A wise man is one who has knowledge and understands how best to use it. There is nothing more wise than to find and then follow the Lord Jesus Christ.

After Jesus was born, "...there came wise men from the east to Jerusalem, saying, Where is he that is born King of the Jews? For we have seen His star in the east, and are come to worship Him" (Matthew 2:1-2).

The Bible foretells nothing of a new star, yet somehow these faithful disciples knew it was coming, and when it appeared they understood it to be the sign of the Messiah. And like all the faithful, they wanted to see Him, be with Him—worship Him. And so, they set out to find Him.

Because light always stirs up darkness, Herod and "all Jerusalem" was "troubled" at the news of the child. Herod "greatly feared" Him as the deliverer spoken of by the prophets, even though He refused to believe and obey. He demanded of the Jews to know where Christ would be born. He was told Bethlehem. Then Herod "called the wise men privily," and learned that the star had appeared almost two years before.

He feigned faith, but his intent was to use the Wise Men to find Jesus and kill Him. And so he sent them on to Bethlehem, saying, "Go and search diligently for the young child; and when ye have found him, bring me word again that I may come and worship Him also" (Matthew 2:8).

As the Wise Men began the short journey to Bethlehem, the star that had begun their long journey in the east reappeared, and beckoned them to follow.

"They rejoiced with exceedingly great joy" to see it again. It "...went before them until it came and stood over where the young child was" (Matthew 2:9).

That star was for them as Christ is for us, a heavenly light so far away, and yet so close and personal. "And when they came into the house, they saw the young child with Mary, His mother, and fell down and worshipped Him..." (Matthew 2:11).

This is why they were called Wise Men. Jesus had "no form nor comeliness, and "no beauty that we should desire Him." He was as ordinary-looking of a toddling child as has ever been born, and yet these grown and wise, seasoned and mature men fell to their knees before him in reverence and meek adoration. They were truly wise for they knew of Him what man cannot know without revelation. This child was their Savior and Redeemer.

"...When they had opened their treasures they gave Him gifts, gold, frankincense, and myrrh" (Matthew 2:11), because those who love the Lord give Him all that they have as well as all that they are.

As the Wise Men settled down to sleep that night, they were "warned of God in a dream not to return to Herod." They rose and departed the country another way. An angel of the Lord then appeared to Joseph in a dream saying "Arise, and take the young child and His mother and flee into Egypt… for Herod will seek the young child to destroy Him'" (Matthew 2:13). The danger was real. Isaiah said Jesus "…would grow up before Him as a tender plant" (Isaiah 53:2).

As a child, Jesus was as subject to cold, hunger, and to death as any other child. When warned of impending danger, immediately Joseph arose and took Jesus and His mother by night and fled into Egypt. Herod was incensed at being so deceived and in an effort to kill the Son of God, he "…sent forth and slew all the children in Bethlehem and in all the coasts thereof from two years old and under…" (Matthew 2:16).

This was the most foolish thing any man could have ever done.

This story is about wise and foolish men.

Fools still ignore and scorn the Son of God.

The wise still seek Him.

If you would be wise in the wisest of all wisdom, "…Ask and it shall be given you; seek, and ye shall find; knock, and it shall be opened unto you" (Matthew 7:7). And remember, just as it was that night for the Wise Men, so will it be for you—the door is still open.

CHAPTER FIFTEEN

A Letter From Dad

It's Christmas time – and you know, this time of year our minds are focused so much on the gifts we need to buy for the ones we love. Well, in light of that, may I share something that happened not too long ago?

I came home from work after a busy day. I went upstairs and dropped my stuff – and then I noticed on my pillow a note, and it was written on that kind of paper, that unique kind of paper, that told me it came from my youngest daughter. I opened it up, and sure enough, it was a note from Shaina.

It said, "Dear Daddy, I miss you. I'm having fun here at school … Can I go to Santa's secret shop? You're gone too much. You are the best daddy in the whole world. Love, Shaina."

Oh – oh, you talk about a payday – I loved it! I called her to me, knelt down on her level, and thanked her for the wonderful note. When I told her I loved her too, she threw her arms around my neck and just hugged me tight. It was a wonderful and tender moment.

Now, a few days later I was with a group of teenagers.

We were chatting casually when, out of genuine curiosity, I asked them, "If you could have anything for Christmas and money was not a consideration, what would it be?"

Well, I have to confess here my shallowness. I expected them to start rambling off all these expensive toys that they would like to have. And to be honest, a few of them did mention some toys they'd like to have. But many, if not most of them, wanted such things as – their families home for the holidays; they wanted to spend time with their families and share experiences with their loved ones. I was surprised by that; I was impressed by that.

One young woman's answer stood out in particular. She's a quiet, pretty young woman.

In response to the question, she said, "Well, I'd want some money for Christmas, and then I'd want a letter from my dad." Well, the money answer I expected, but the letter from dad – I was taken back by that, and I asked her why she would want that. I mean, I figured of all things that a teenager would want least from her parents, a sentimental letter would be that last thing.

Well, she explained that her father, at least once a year, writes her a letter in which he opens his heart, and tells her that he loves her. The letters have become a cherished tradition for her. In them, Dad bears his testimony, shares the experiences of his own life, and gives her guidance, and tells her what he expects from her.

I couldn't believe what I was hearing.

"You mean to tell me, of all the things you could have, you would most want a letter from your dad?"

"Yes," she said, and she meant it!

You know something? Maybe our loved ones really don't want the gifts that come out of stores this year as much as they want the gifts that come out of the heart – the gifts of memories.

Now, as a related thought, it was recently explained to me what WWJD meant. I had never heard that before. It means What Would Jesus Do? Well, may I suggest something new for Christmas this year? How about WWJG? – What Would Jesus Give?

Merry Christmas to you.

CHAPTER SIXTEEN

The Babe of Bethlehem

Jesus, the Babe of Bethlehem — He lived, and today He lives again and watches over us as Mary once watched over Him. Where once He was cradled as a helpless babe in a lowly manger, now He reigns as King of Kings and Lord of Lords in courts of eternal glory.

He was once tender and fragile, helpless, as susceptible to death and injury as any other, but now He is all-powerful and all-wise, the author and finisher of our faith.

He was born the Daystar, the light, and the life of the world. Where this world was dark and cruel on the night He came, He will make it glorious and perfect.

He came as a babe, but He was God, sent to a world that had forgotten God. And through Him, all may be one with God.

Like every other baby ever born, His memory was veiled and His innocence sweet. He descended from a heavenly throne and never stopped that plunging descent until he was raised upon the cross. But now, He stands above us all with hands outstretched, inviting us to be one with Him where He is. He was comprehended by none, but now He comprehends and loves us all.

Be assured that as angels announced with heart and voice His coming once, they will do so again. Shepherds were His witnesses then, and they still are. He came once as a suffering servant, He will come again, this time a conquering King.

At His birth, He was adored by few, hated by some, and ignored by most, but no one can ignore Him now. He is our Savior and Redeemer, meriting our worship, and universal adoration.

He was born a subject of Rome, a slave to Caesar's whim, but He rose as the King to conquer all, even death and hell.

Mary, His mother, loved Him and from Bethlehem to Calvary she never left Him. Today, some of the best parents in the history of this world are here. He never leaves them. If only we understood how concerned about such matters He really is. I want you to know our faith in Him is never unappreciated. Our prayers are never ignored.

Mary wrapped Him in swaddling clothes when He was born, but now, those swaddling clothes of the commoner are the resplendent white robes of eternal glory, and He will give them to us.

At His first coming, only Mary and Joseph saw to His comfort and care. The world turned a cold heart. But we have His promise—when He comes again, His heart will be turned to those who have waited long for Him. They will come forth, His loving kindness burning in their heart's memory forever.

As Joseph and Mary took Him to Egypt and saved him from Herod's hate and man's envy, so too, He will take us out of Egypt--the world, to another world where hate and envy ne'er annoy.

He was born to a stable and raised to mansions of glory. On that first Christmas night, no one understood and so no one made room for Him, but now, His heart, broad as the heavens, swells wide as eternity. There is, thank God, room for us all.

He was born to us, but He is the Savior of worlds without number. He was born Mary's Son, He rose Mary's King!

CHAPTER SEVENTEEN

Christmas and the Golden Rule

Two millennia ago angels sang out in heavenly triumph, "Glory to God in the highest, and on earth peace, good will toward men" (Luke 2:14). The Savior is still the Prince of Peace. So, why is there so little good will now?

Why in our day do we live with wars and rumors of war? Why do we have pestilence and plagues approaching epidemic proportions? Explain to me, if you please, the logic of weapons of mass destruction. Why? Terrorists, why do we have them and their twisted minds?

Why is it that entire populations will be decimated this next year by AIDS and starvation? Why do earthquakes, volcanoes, hurricanes, and other disasters increase and ruin lives and property? Why is it that there are those who rape the land for greed?

What has happened to us? Has our world gone crazy? Why is there so much anger and hate? Why are there so many people so unhappy and so much heartbreak and abuse in our homes? It is because we have not understood!

There is a doctrine of the Prince of Peace so little considered, but so powerful in scope that if applied would literally change our world. Other than his Atonement, there is perhaps no other teaching so closely connected with the Lord's ministry. The awesome power to change our lives, our families, and our world lies in a simple formula.

He said, "...all things whatsoever ye would that men should do to you, do ye even so to them..." (Matthew 7:12). As the love of men waxes cold, think of the global warming of hearts that would come if all men treated each other as they would want to be treated? How should I treat my wife? Like I would want to be treated if I were her. To do this, I must place myself in her mind and heart and then act.

I know that some will scoff and say that this is nothing more than words in the wind or pie in the sky; that it's not practical, but please explain to me how war is practical. Where have threats, hate, envy, and greed ever made the world better? I'm not saying there's not a time to fight, but if we are going to fight, let's do it on the Lord's terms.

When an adulterous woman was thrown at His feet to be condemned, He wouldn't. When others shunned publicans and harlots, He wouldn't. When the disciples wanted to send away a pleading Gentile woman, He wouldn't. While everyone else ran from a man possessed with a legion of devils, Jesus went to him and healed him. And, as for vengeance, when He suffered and bled in Gethsemane, we caused that. We hurt Him in a way unimaginable, yet He didn't come out of that bitter and resenting us, but loved us all the more.

They beat him, mocked Him, spit in his face, and pierced His brow with thorns. They twisted his words, clamored for His blood, and stripped Him of his garments in public. Yet, with quiet dignity, He stood it, returning good for evil, love for hate. He did not give them what they wanted but gave them what they really needed. As the Romans crucified Him, He asked that they be forgiven.

The golden rule, not the rule of gold, was the rule of His life. Can anyone doubt that He changed the world for good? My friends, returning hate for hate only breeds more hate.

Where are you Christmas? Why have you gone away? Why can't we keep you all year long? We can!

The Spirit of Christmas is the Spirit of Christ. This year, don't lose it. Love thy neighbor as thyself, is the law, and the golden rule is how we do it. This year, give the real gift of gold, the golden rule. Shake this world to its core. Start with your family, and let love become a global epidemic. It will work! I promise. Peace and good will will come. Merry Christmas, and oh, hear me—God Bless us to do this before it's too late!

Chapter Eighteen

Christmas Symbolism

Nothing about the Christmas story, I want you to know, is accidental or haphazard. Every part of that beautifully simple story is a story in and of itself, and all of it bears witness to the living reality of our Savior.

For example: During the Savior's ministry, He was called the Bread of Life. Bread is now, as it was then, the staff of life. It's the mainstay of our diet. Jesus, the Bread of Life, was born in Bethlehem. Bethlehem means House of Bread.

Jesus is the Good Shepherd; and who was it that was privileged first to see Him and proclaim His birth? – Shepherds, those who tended the flocks.

Many scriptures refer to Jesus as the Lamb of God, He who was to die for our sins. Well, those flocks that were on the hills around Bethlehem that night – more than likely they were Temple Lambs destined for sacrifice for the sins of the people on the altars of the Temple.

How fitting it is that He who was called by John the Bright and Morning Star should have that as His sign – A new star, brighter than any other in the heavens.

And again, laid in a manger, a symbol of His lowliness, the Savior's beginnings were as humble and as lowly as any child that has ever been born. How appropriate that is when later He commanded us to become as children – meek, lowly, and humble.

What about the angel who proclaimed the birth of our Savior, Gabriel? That same Gabriel, as Noah centuries earlier, was the Savior of the human family from the waters of the flood.

Also, in the Christmas story, there are repeated references to David, that the Christ-child would be born David's son in David's city, and receive David's throne. Well, what of this David? – In the Old Testament, David was called a man after the Lord's own heart. He was Israel's mightiest king. It was he who in power and glory freed Israel from political and spiritual bondage, united her tribes, and gave her the greatest prosperity and freedom that she ever enjoyed.

Just think about this for a moment. He whose birth brought a moment of peace will return again to this earth to bring a millennium of peace.

Well, there's more, much more within this story to tell. But I close with this: the wise men from the east followed a comparatively small light from a star, and they found Him. Now today, if we will follow that small gentle light from within, the light of the Holy Ghost, we will find Him, who is the light and the life of the world, even the Son of God.

CHAPTER NINETEEN

Christmas in the Americas

You'll recall that the night the Savior was born, angels sang in the heavens, "Glory to God in the highest, and on Earth peace good will toward men"(Luke 2:14). Peace! Think about that word, peace. Of all the words the angels could have said to tell us what the birth of a Savior would mean, they said peace. Jesus is the Prince of Peace. Christmas is peace. Now, if you wouldn't mind, may I share a story with you from another land a long time ago?

The nation was torn apart. Contention and hate filled the land, dividing the people. On one hand, there were those, few in number, who believed that Christ would come. He would be born to this earth. But then, there were those, by far the majority, who refused to believe in the words of the prophets and would not accept the coming of Christ.

Every sign and miracle that was manifest was explained away by the unbelievers, either as a coincidence, or a lucky guess by the prophets. Religion came to be seen as a wicked and seditious tradition. The persecution against the believers began as simple, annoying gossip but then grew into deadly threats and violence.

Suddenly, there arose a group of the non-believers who declared that the time was past for the Messiah to come, and their words raged throughout the land like a summer forest fire, causing a tremendous uproar. People caught hold of them, joined in, and while the people of God held firm in the faith that Christ would come, the wicked plotted their death. A date was set aside and plans were made to execute the people of God for their belief in the coming of Christ.

Finally, it came to a climax. The next day those who had believed in the ancient traditions of the coming of Christ were to be murdered by their own countrymen. While the wicked prepared to murder, the righteous prayed mightily all that day — and then, miracle of miracles.

That night, as the sun went down below the horizon, it didn't get dark. To the utter astonishment of all the people, the land remained as light as though it were mid-day. A new and glorious star arose in the heavens that night and the people recognized it as the long-promised sign of the birth of Christ. While the faithful rejoiced in their deliverance, the unbelievers fell to the earth in utter astonishment. Fear and the spirit of repentance came upon them.

The next morning as the sun arose, the light of faith arose with it. And this is interesting… All thoughts of murder and contention were swept away by the spirit of the Lord that filled the hearts of the people across the land. Peace and goodwill reigned in their hearts.

The day was Christmas. That day, on the other side of the world, He who would be called the Prince of Peace was born of Mary and laid in a manger.

It intrigues me that even in his birth, Jesus, who would someday be Savior of us all, even as a tiny babe saved his people, the Nephites.

My dear friends, of all things, Christmas is peace! Christ is peace! Now, as then, all who will let the Daystar arise in their hearts will know for themselves of assurity the blessing invoked by the angels that first night. To have faith in Christ is to have peace on earth, good will toward men.

CHAPTER TWENTY

A Savior

Christmas is a season for gifts.

May I speak of the greatest single gift that has ever been given?

Consider these words: "For God so loved the world, that he gave his only begotten Son, that whosoever believeth in him should not perish, but have everlasting life" (John 3:16). What a gift!

On the night those shepherds, just and holy men they were, kept watch over their flock by night, an angel of the Lord appeared in glory to them and announced, "For unto you is born this day in the city of David a Savior, which is Christ the Lord" (Luke 2:11) – a Savior, the gift of a Savior.

You know, for most of my life, I have not fully appreciated this title of the Master. Maybe I still don't. But I know that my understanding has recently begun to change. May I share an experience?

Years ago, while at the hospital for the birth of one of our children, things had progressed to that point where delivery of the child was only moments away. I was as tense as a cat. I watched the monitoring nurse doing routine checks, and noticed suddenly her facial expression changed. I sensed instantly that something was wrong.

A call went out, a doctor ran into the room, and confirmed that the baby was in serious trouble. Normal delivery would kill her. Even though it was an unlikely time of the day, the call went throughout the hospital, and a team of doctors and nurses was scrambled. All the while, one doctor and one nurse worked with great effort and skill to save my baby's life. Within minutes of the first alarm, an emergency cesarean section was performed and the baby was saved.

The nurses took me and took the baby down to the nursery where she was cleaned and examined. When they were done, I had the choice privilege of holding her for the first time. As I sat in that chair and looked into that little face, I was overcome with one of the most profound feelings of gratitude I have ever felt in my life, gratitude to my dear wife for her sacrifice, gratitude to God for a beloved and perfect new daughter, and not the least, gratitude to trained self-sacrificing doctors and nurses, saviors if you will of my little daughter.

Now every so often I look at her, and I remember how I almost lost her, and how she was saved from sure death, and I'm reminded in a deeper and a more personal way of what it means to have the gift of a Savior, which is Christ the Lord.

CHAPTER TWENTY-ONE

Unto You

You know, Christmas means a lot of different things to different people. I recently had an experience that still leaves me wondering – a little awestruck.

My morning began in front of a group of teenagers who told me of their various struggles to know if the Gospel of Jesus Christ was really true. The darkness and doubt they were wrestling with was evident in their faces. I was their teacher. What could I do? I know it's true. I could tell them it's true, but how could I give them what I felt?

Later that morning, a young woman came into my office and broke down and cried as she told of her unconverted father, and what his lack of faith was doing to her and to their family. My heart went out to her as she told me how much she wanted her father to change, to repent, and make their family a forever family. But she also told me how much she doubted that that would ever happen.

Another young woman sitting right beside her friend, whose family has recently been torn apart by a terrible divorce, told me what a struggle it was to go on after her perfect world had been shattered.

And then, just before she left, she asked me this question, "How can I forgive my dad for what he's done?"

What would you say?

I know a little of how deep pain like that can be, and how hard it is to change a heart full of bitterness and anger. It isn't something you can just smile away. These aren't problems you can solve by putting a goal in your day planner. There's no pithy advice that makes all of this better. This is real! These are real problems and real people.

Well, my day wasn't over yet. That afternoon, I met with the parents of a young man who was rebelling against all that he'd been taught. I knew these parents and I knew this young man. I felt so sorry for them. I knew that they've prayed, and cried and agonized over this son that they love so much, and yet he did not seem to care. It occurred to me that no matter how much they loved that son, they couldn't change him; they couldn't force him. I didn't know how to change him either.

I got home that afternoon. There was a letter waiting for me – from the state prison. It came from an inmate, a former student, who in high school had 'gotten in' with bad friends who had led him into trouble. He abandoned the religion of his upbringing, and soon his life was spiraling out of control and not even he could stop it. Addiction and criminal behavior finally landed him before a court where he was convicted, sentenced, and sent to prison.

He wrote to me the following in a letter: "… What I want to ask you, Brother Rawson, is if you would pray for me.

Would you pray for me to be able to get probation, and be able to live with my son and wife, and not be tempted with drugs? Please! I pray every night for the Lord to change me, and take the hate and any other evil out of me." "Why," he said, "did I start so soon?"

I do hope and pray that he changes. But I also know that the power to change him does not lie within me, nor even within him. There are those who would say that such problems as I've encountered today are hopeless, that people can't change in truly fundamental ways. Some would say that there – there's no power strong enough to heel the kinds of problems that I encountered today. I don't believe that! It's not true!

Now here's why I tell you that story. The irony is what I was teaching in my classes to my students on that very same day. I was teaching Luke 2, 'The Christmas Story.'

You remember that after the Christ-child was born, the scripture records that, "… there were in the same country shepherds abiding in the field[s], keeping watch over their flock[s] by night. And, lo, the angel of the Lord came upon them, and the glory of the Lord shone round about them: and they were sore afraid. And the angel said unto them, Fear not: for, behold, I bring you good tidings of great joy, which shall be to all people. For unto you is born this day in the city of David – a Savior, which is Christ the Lord" (Luke 2:8-11).

You know, there are over a hundred names and titles for Jesus in the scriptures. I find it interesting that the angel said – and notice how He said this, it's so personal – "… unto you …," – not the world – "… unto you is born … a Savior, …".

My friends, that's what Christmas means. It's the gift of one who is mighty to save, to save our families, our children, our parents, our friends, our nation, our world, and yes, even us from ourselves.

Merry Christmas to you – all of you, and to those of you who need Him, remember what He said.

"I, the Lord, am bound when ye do what I say; …"

(D & C 82:10).

God bless you.

CHAPTER TWENTY-TWO

Boyhood of Jesus

The Lord Jesus Christ was the one perfect being this world has ever known. When He said "follow me," it was not just in where He went, but in the way He went. From His childhood, He was the perfect example.

An angel of the Lord appeared to Joseph in Egypt and told him that it was safe to take Mary and Jesus back to Israel. It was his intention to return to Bethlehem, but when he learned that Herod's son ruled there, he feared going back. Directed again by the angel, he went to an obscure Galilean village called Nazareth (Matthew 2:19-23).

 And there Jesus grew up with his brethren. He was the oldest of five brothers, James, Joses, Simon and Judas, and at least two sisters (Matthew 13:55-56).

At the age of twelve, Jesus traveled with His parents to Jerusalem for the feast of the Passover. When they set out for home, Jesus stayed back. Three days later, they found Him in the Temple, teaching the doctors and answering their questions. It was an amazing spectacle, both to His audience and His parents, to see this mere boy teaching the gospel to the wisest of His day.

"Son," His mother said, "why hast thou thus dealt with us? Behold thy father and I have sought thee sorrowing." (Luke 2:48)

"How is it that ye sought me," he said, "wist ye not that I must be about my father's business?" (Luke 2:49) He had tarried by design to teach and bring souls unto God. Where else should his parents have looked for Him than in the Temple—His Father's house.

Nevertheless, He obeyed His parents and went home with them. By the age of twelve, Jesus knew He was God's son, not Joseph's son. However, Jesus was born with no memory of his former glory. Like every other child, He grew line upon line and precept upon precept, increasing in wisdom, except, He grew until no man on earth was wise enough to teach Him. He spoke and acted like no other man before or since (JST Matthew 2:23). And yet, as He grew powerful, He also increased in favor with God and man (Luke 2:52).

He always did those things that pleased His Heavenly Father and consequently, the grace of God was upon Him (Luke 2:40), and never left Him. Similarly, He understood love and by that power men loved Him.

Jesus knew who He was and what He was born to do and yet for 30 years, He was the carpenter's son, working under Joseph. All the while waiting—preparing, growing in strength, wisdom, and spirituality. And when it was time, he came out of Galilee to Jordan, unto John to be baptized, having prepared Himself spiritually, intellectually, physically, and socially, just as we must do if we would go where He went, and become as He was.

CHAPTER TWENTY-THREE

Samuel and the Christ

When Jesus was born in Bethlehem, it appears that the sacred event passed generally unnoticed. But, on the other side of the world in the Americas, everyone noticed. That first Christmas in the new world was a monumental moment that changed history. Of all people to be the Lord's witness of his impending birth, it was a despised Lamanite, named Samuel. Oh, what a prophet he was! This is the story.

They wouldn't let him into the city. He was not their kind and his message was offensive. Undeterred, he got upon the high walls of the city of Zarahemla and shouted the tidings to all. The Messiah was coming, and Samuel was sent to call them to repentance and get them ready.

And then, to place a seal on his words, he said, "This will I give unto you for a sign at the time of his coming; for behold, there shall be great lights in heaven, insomuch that in the night before he cometh there shall be no darkness, insomuch that it shall appear unto man as if it was day. Therefore there shall be one day and a night and a day, as if it were one day…and it shall be the night before he is born" (Helaman 14:3-4).

Then he stunned them further by announcing "…there shall a new star arise, such an one as ye never have beheld…" (Helaman 14:5).

Though many people believed Samuel, the more part of them rejected him, even attempting to kill him. His prophecy spread across the land, and people began to count the days.

Five years came and went. Because some thought the time had passed, a great uproar was made throughout the land— even death threats against the believers. Then it happened. The sun went down, but it did not get dark. It remained throughout that night as light as at noonday. On schedule, the sun rose again, as did the new star. The people were so astonished that they fell to the earth and knew, according to the prophecy, that Christ—the Daystar would be born that day.

The people were converted. Most of them believed and great peace settled over the land. Then, to our astonishment, less than five years later, "…the people began to forget those signs and wonders… insomuch that they began to be hard in their hearts and blind in their minds, and began to disbelieve all which they had heard and seen" (3 Nephi 2:1). There it is! In their minds, they knew what had happened, but in their hearts, they refused to feel what it meant. Now today, we know what happened 2000 years ago, but do we believe it—do we really feel it? Christmas has to happen in the heart or it's just another busy holiday. It is a good thing to know the Christmas story and a much better thing to know Christ. Open your heart to the Holy Spirit of Christmas.

CHAPTER TWENTY- FOUR

Alma at Gideon

His people had gone astray, their focus of faith shifting from the God who redeemed them to the wealth He gave them. It was 83 B.C. when Alma set out to reclaim the people of the Church from their crippling pride.

He traveled first to the land of Zarahemla and after much affliction and sorrow, was able to bring his people to repentance. From there, he crossed the River Sidon into the valley of Gideon, and began to teach. "…There be many things to come;" he said to them, "and behold, there is one thing more important than they all for behold, the time is not far distant that the Redeemer liveth and cometh among his people" (Alma 7:7).

I have wondered why these ancient ones spoke so often of that sacred Christmas story so many years before it happened. What did it mean to them?

Alma continued, "…behold, the kingdom of heaven is at hand, and the Son of God cometh upon the face of the earth. And behold, he shall be born of Mary at Jerusalem which is the land of our forefathers, she being a virgin and a precious and chosen vessel, who shall be overshadowed and conceive by the power of the Holy Ghost, and bring forth a son, yea, even the Son of God" (Alma 7:9-10).

Think of it, the Son of Almighty God was coming to earth to live among men! What greater tidings could there be than that? As Alma continued, it became evident why this story was so important to him.

"And he shall go forth, suffering pains and afflictions and temptations of every kind;... And he will take upon him death that he may loose the bands of death... which bind his people; and he will take upon him their infirmities, that his bowels may be filled with mercy, according to the flesh, that he may know according to the flesh how to succor his people according to their infirmities" (Alma 7:11-12).

Jesus was born among men to suffer all that man can suffer, that his own soul would be filled with mercy and succor. He is verily just what the angel announced him to be at Bethlehem, "For unto you is born this day in the city of David a Savior, which is Christ the Lord" (Luke 2:11).

Alma told the Christmas story to awaken the faith of his people in a Savior who would come and be one of them and could help them as no other could. He wanted them to "...have faith on the Lamb of God, who taketh away the sins of the world, who is mighty to save and cleanse from all unrighteousness" (Alma 7:14). Christmas means so much more when we look beyond the cradle to the Cross—and from there, to the empty tomb.

CHAPTER TWENTY- FIVE

Mary

From all of our Father's daughters, Mary, the mother of the Savior, was chosen before she was born to be the mother of God's almighty Son (Alma 7:10).

Mary was the noblest and greatest of all of our Father's daughters (Luke 1:28). Her name, an exalted position, was known centuries before she was ever born (Mosiah 3:8). She was of the tribe of Judah, and through her blood, the scepter of leadership would pass to Shiloh. The Lord's mother was of the royal line of King David, thus making her a princess (Luke 1:27).

Her name, Mary, is the Greek form of the Hebrew name Miriam, which means exalted (Bible Dictionary; Miriam).

In a land ripe with apostasy and corruption, she was clean and pure, and worthy before the Lord (Mosiah 3:8).

By her obedience, she attained a place of special favor with God. He loved her, and He counted Mary as precious. Even the mighty Gabriel said, "Hail thou that art highly favored, blessed art thou among women" (Luke 1:28; Alma 7:10).

Mary was an extraordinarily beautiful woman. In fact, of all virgins, she was, the prophet Nephi said, the most beautiful and fair ever to live (1 Nephi 11:15). And, what of her being a virgin? Jesus was born of a woman that there could never be even the slightest doubt or disputation whose son He was. With Gabriel's call, Mary responded, "…Behold the handmaid of the Lord; be it unto me according to thy word…" (Luke 1:38).

For all that Mary was great, Mary was humble, and I further believe that by that declaration never was so much accepted by any woman in so few words. Even though Mary was young, she was not naïve nor uninformed. There was a maturity about her. Consider these words: "…my spirit hath rejoiced in God my Savior" (Luke 1:47), she said when she met Elizabeth. Mary understood the prophecies, and she had a relationship with God even before she bore His Son.

I find it inspiring that when Mary was with child, and it came to a choice between standing in public favor with Joseph as her husband or standing alone as the mother of God's Son, facing the possibility of public shame and even punishment, she chose the lonelier course. She was a woman who was true at all times. Moreover, she bore the ordeal of the journey to Bethlehem, and giving birth in the manger – and there is not the least inference in the revelations anywhere that Mary ever murmured, doubted, or wavered.

While others announced far and wide the birth of her chosen son, I find it interesting that Mary kept a disciplined and sacred silence. Mary saw and understood many things which she did not share. Through her son, the law of Moses would be fulfilled. Yet Mary complied with that law's every command after His birth.

She was a woman of courage and determination. You'll remember that Simeon proclaimed in the Temple,

"Yea, a sword shall pierce through thy own soul also..." (Luke 2:35). Mary was as close to Jesus as any human being could be. What mother does not suffer at the suffering of her babes? All that ever came upon Him, even to the spear that pierced Him at the end, came in some measure upon her. Yet, she bore it valiantly to the very end.

Mary was loyal and devoted to Joseph. Even though she was the woman chosen, and the woman of great favor, she obeyed Joseph's dreams and followed Him into Egypt, and later into Nazareth.

Similarly, she had absolute faith in her son. When she needed a miracle of wine, she came to Him. How it must have hurt her when her other sons, James, Joses, Simon and Judah, did not accept their older brother Jesus for who and what He was (Matthew 13:55-57). Her loyalty to her son was total. In His infancy, she would protect Him; in His manhood, He would watch over her; in His Godhood, He would exalt her. All generations, now and forever, deservedly call her blessed among women.

Thank God for Mary. There is so much more about that holy woman that we do not know and cannot say, that will someday be revealed to the faithful as one of the greatest women ever to live.

Merry Christmas.

CHAPTER TWENTY- SIX

Simeon and Anna

I heard it said recently, if all you know is what you see with your natural eyes and hear with your natural ears, then you will not know very much. Those who live by the Holy Ghost see, hear, and know much more than those of the world can enjoy,as this Christmas story illustrates.

Forty days after the Savior's birth, Joseph and Mary brought him to the Temple in Jerusalem. Since the Passover, every firstborn son in Israel belonged to the Lord. Joseph and Mary made an offering in their poverty of two turtledoves to redeem him. To see it another way, Joseph made a sacrificial offering to redeem his son, just as Heavenly Father would later make a sacrificial offering of His Son and redeem all mankind.

"And, behold, there was a man in Jerusalem, whose name was Simeon; and the same man was just and devout, waiting for the consolation of Israel: and the Holy Ghost was upon him. And it was revealed unto him by the Holy Ghost that he should not see death, before he had seen the Lord's Christ" (Luke 2:25-26).

On that day, and at that time, the Spirit led Simeon into the crowded temple just as Joseph and Mary arrived there. With all of Jerusalem as an audience, the Holy Ghost identified Jesus to Simeon. He came and took the blessed infant in his arms. "Lord," he said in humble praise, "now lettest thou thy servant depart in peace, according to the word: For mine eyes have seen thy salvation, Which thou hast prepared before the face of all people; a light to lighten the Gentiles and the glory of thy people Israel" (Luke 2:29-31).

Simeon was joyously happy because that day which he had lived for, for so long, had come. Joseph and Mary "...marvelled at those things which were spoken of him" (Luke 2:33). Seldom does the Lord reveal all His word at once. Line upon line, revelation comes incrementally and in packets to the faithful. Joseph and Mary are still learning who their Son really is.

Then, Simeon turned to Mary and spoke to her sensitive soul. "This child," he said, as if in "warning," "is set for the fall and rising again of many in Israel; and for a sign which shall be spoken against" (Luke 2:34). Your Son, Mary, will reveal the hearts of all men. He will be both loved and hated. His name will be had for good and evil among all men. Those who love light and truth will come in reverence to Him and will rise with him. Those who love darkness rather than light will be exposed, and they will hate Him and they will fall. "Yea," he continued, as if in prophetic illustration, "a sword shall pierce through Him, to the wounding of thine own soul also" (JST, Luke 2:35).

What kind of statement is that to make to a mother in the joy of a new son? No wonder people ignore this part of the Christmas story. But, in this prophecy is embodied the real meaning of Christmas and the Savior's life. As Elder Jeffrey R. Holland put it, "It is life at the other end of the manger that gives this moment of nativity in Bethlehem its ultimate meaning" (Elder Jeffrey R. Holland, BYU-I devotional 12-1-98).

Gethsemane, Golgotha, and the Garden Tomb give Christmas its real meaning and joy, and the old man about to die, Simeon, and Anna who came moments later, knew that. All of us have and will fall, but praise God from whom all blessings flow—joy to the world, indeed, for we can rise again.

When we see Christmas as Simeon did, the season becomes one of worship, and the joy and peace last all year. The best gifts become those that express the most love for God and man.

CHAPTER TWENTY- SEVEN

Grace to Grace

Reluctantly, we must let the Christmas holiday go, but don't let that Spirit go. Do as Jesus did after His first Christmas.

When it was safe, Joseph brought Mary and Jesus out of Egypt and settled them in Nazareth of Galilee. Christmas was over and the mortal probation of God's Son was underway.

Mortality is indeed a probation. Each of us was given a body, mind, and heart, and the time, means, and a commandment to improve all three. With these gifts, we live life to love God and our fellow men. It was the same for Jesus and more so, for where "...much is given much is required" (D&C 82:3). Will the progress be slow? Will it take time and patience? Jesus waited thirty years before He was ready.

Jesus "...served under his father... (JST Matthew 3:25), Joseph the carpenter, thereby, He not only grew physically but he waxed strong. Jesus was a strong man.

There is indescribable joy in mastering and strengthening the body.

Jesus also grew spiritually. Luke says he "...waxed strong in Spirit...and the grace of God was upon Him" (Luke 2:40), and that he "increased in... favor with God..." (Luke 2:52). Jesus was close to His Father. As we study, obey, and pray, so will it be with us, and it will feel so good.

Luke also says Jesus "...increased in wisdom..." (Luke 2:52). Wisdom is vision and power. The Savior developed His mind to an astonishing degree, becoming wiser than any man in His generation, even Solomon himself. It is for us as it was for Him, we must pray and study.

It is fascinating to know that even in His youth, Jesus "... spake not as other men, neither could He be taught; for He needed not that any man should teach him" (JST, Matthew 3:25). He was so far above every man in every way, yet, as He increased in favor with God, He also increased in favor with man. People liked Him. In stark contrast to the hate and crucifixion at the end of His life, at the beginning, He was loved and favored by those who knew Him. He loved and was loved, as I hope happens with us.

Do as Jesus did after His first Christmas. Grow in mind, body, and spirit. Open your heart and love God and man. As we let Him in, He takes us from grace to grace, higher and higher in power and perfection of mind, body, and heart until that perfect day.

CHAPTER TWENTY-EIGHT

Grateful for Gratitude

We are commanded, my friends, to live in thanksgiving daily, always returning thanks for whatsoever we receive.

Why? Does God need our gratitude? No, we do.

I will never forget the Christmas of 2006. Shaina wanted a keyboard for Christmas.

I mean she really wanted a keyboard! We looked at used ones, but the cost was too much. Every chance she got though, Shaina would play one and just dream. As young ones often do, she pestered us incessantly wanting a keyboard.

Finally, I sat her down and explained, "We just can't afford it." But then I said, "Be patient though, my dear, and I promise I'll get you one. All good things come to those who wait."

She never said another word about it, but we knew she was mightily disappointed. Then – for some reason, we felt as though we should make the sacrifice and get it for her. We did.

So, on Christmas morning, we opened our presents, but the keyboard was hidden away. Shaina seemed content and happy with what she'd received, and I noticed that.

Then when all the presents were opened, Mom led the family into the laundry room. There was the prized drum set for Hannah, the guitar for Travis and Sherise, and the keyboard for Shaina.

Hannah screamed and danced through the house. Travis and Sherise picked up the guitar and began to "plink." But Shaina – she took one look at the keyboard, screamed with excitement, and then turned and buried her face in my chest, and just held on to me. But at first, I thought she was laughing. Then I realized she was crying – not just crying, she was sobbing – with joy. For a long moment, she just held onto me and cried, and cried, and cried. No one noticed, but – Dad was crying too – as I do every time I think about that moment. I'm not sure there's anything a father appreciates more than a truly grateful child. Her tears of gratitude were more than ample payment for our sacrifice.

"… God so loved the world, that he gave his only begotten Son …" (John 3:16).

Just imagine the joy the Father and the Son will share with us when we with true understanding fall at their feet, and bathe those feet with tears of joy and gratitude. That child who seeks to understand what has been done for them, and never stops expressing it, is the child that a parent loves to bless.

So, practice your gratitude like Shaina practices piano. It is music to our Father and is the mark of a cultivated mind. To perfect gratitude is to master the natural man, and to know God.

CHAPTER TWENTY-NINE

The Christmas Gift of Freedom

Does God care about human freedom? Can a man be saved in bondage? Now, these are important questions. By way of an answer, I have an unusual Christmas story I would like to share with you.

It was December 1776. The tattered remnants of George Washington's Continental Army were camped in the open on the banks of the Delaware River. Where once they had been some 20,000 in number, bold and strong, now they were less than 6,000. Where once they had soundly defeated the British at Lexington and Concord, now they were a decimated band running for their lives across the frozen New Jersey landscape with the British in hot, humiliating pursuit.

And now here they were, huddled around fires to keep from freezing, their rations reduced to starvation subsistence, even living on tree bark. Their inadequate clothing was nothing more than filthy rags hanging on emaciated bodies. They were dejected and defeated, as beaten psychologically as they were physically. And yet, on this ragtag group of men hung all the hopes of the

American Revolution. This was the army. They were all that stood between America and avowed British tyranny.

Consider, if you will, General Washington. At this time, he was about as burdened a man as ever lived. Many were calling for his resignation, even within the Continental Congress. Officers within his own command were openly murmuring against him, and positioning to replace him. Desertions within the ranks of his army were rampant and daily. Here he stood on the banks of the Delaware with an army seemingly too weak to fight, feeling the weight – and carrying the blame of the American plight.

Meanwhile, across the river in Trenton, safe and warm, were the Hessian mercenaries left by General Howe to hold Washington's pitiful army at bay. He could have finished them at any time, but it was widely known that on December 31st the enlistments of Washington's army expired. The men would go home. The British saw no need to attack and finish them off. Cold, starvation, desertion – they would finish the fight for them. All the British and the Germans needed to do was sit and watch while the American Revolution collapsed upon itself, and the dream – that arrogant dream of American freedom – to die with it. I don't need to tell you, this was a monumental historical moment.

At one of the lowest points, Thomas Paine came into camp, talking and mingling with the soldiers. He was deeply moved by their plight, and sat down and, according to some, penned a pamphlet called "The American Crisis" on the head of a drum. These are some of those words he wrote at that critical time:

"These are the times that try men's souls: the summer soldier and the sunshine patriot will, in this crisis, shrink from the service of his country, but he that stands it now, deserves the love and thanks of man and woman. Tyranny, like hell, is not easily conquered, yet we have this consolation with us, that the harder the conflict, the more glorious the triumph. What we obtain too cheap, we esteem too lightly: – tis dearness only that gives everything its value. Heaven knows how to put a proper price upon its goods; and it would be strange indeed, if so celestial an article as Freedom should not be highly rated" (The American Crisis I, December 19, 1776).

These words caused a storm through America. To the credit of the man and the power of heaven that moved him, Washington was inspired by these words, and by the powers of Heaven. He did not lie down in defeat. He rose from his knees, gathered his ragged and beaten army, and in the face of a terrible howling blizzard crossed the Delaware on Christmas night, 1776. Several thousand men, cannon, and horses were ferried across the ice-choked, black waters of the Delaware. From there, Washington marched his men nine miles to Trenton, leaving bloody footprints in the snow as he went   in weather literally so cold that men froze to death the moment they sat down. At dawn, Washington did the impossible with the incapable. He attacked Trenton and the unsuspecting Hessians, and captured the men and the city – and lost not a single man in the battle.

Inspired by that timely victory, the faltering fight for American freedom regained its momentum. Men reenlisted, volunteers came, allies joined, and the battle for freedom went on to victory. Washington, over the next few days, captured Princeton and sufficient supplies to carry his men through the winter safely quartered at Morristown.

But oh, think about that moment – when it would have been so easy to give up the fight and quit. Thank God for that man. Thank God for those men! Little did they know how much their sacrifice would change the course of human history, and change our lives. I tell you – with all of my soul, the cause of freedom is the cause of Christ. His birth signaled the opening of the prison doors. No man can be saved in bondage, political or spiritual. We must be free in heart and in person.

Praise be to God for an oft-forgotten Christmas gift given by humble men and women at great cost. Thanks be to God and Merry Christmas!

About The Author

Glenn Rawson has been telling inspirational stories for over 30 years. His stories started as a way to teach and share with his family and a few close friends.

Glenn Rawson was born and raised in Idaho. He grew up on a cattle ranch, and to this day still carries a little bit of cowboy in him. When he was 18 years old, he joined The Church of Jesus Christ of Latter-day Saints and later served a mission in Iowa. He graduated from Brigham Young University with a degree in Wildlife and Range Science, and later from Idaho State University with a master's degree in education. He spent almost 20 years as a seminary and institute teacher.

In 1997, he began writing and producing stories for the radio. His stories continue to be heard on numerous stations around the country. That work in radio later turned into production work for church specials. Then, in 2008, he joined with KJZZ television in Salt Lake City and the Joseph Smith Papers team to produce a weekly documentary television series entitled, The Joseph Smith Papers. In 2010, he teamed with Dennis Lyman and Bryant Bush to produce a new series called History of the Saints. Glenn and his wife Debbie have seven children and seventeen grandchildren. They live in Utah. Glenn is a simple storyteller whose goal is to inspire and lift people.

In addition to traveling around the world, he has studied the scriptures extensively and is happy to present this book to you.

For information about receiving weekly stories and other books available, please visit

glennrawsonstories.com or **historyofthesaints.org.**